GW01388474

THE DOERS

Roz Tucker-Shaw
Illustrated by Scott Ross

THE DOERS

Roz Tucker-Shaw
Illustrated by Scott Ross

THE DOERS
Copyright © Roz Tucker-Shaw 2010
All rights reserved

No part of this book may be reproduced in any form by photocopying or any electronic or mechanical means, including information storage or retrieval systems, without permission in writing from both the copyright owner and the publisher of the book

ISBN 978-184426-908-2

First published 2010 by Fastprint Publishing, Peterborough, England.

An environmentally friendly book printed and bound in England by
www.printondemand-worldwide.com

PEFC
PEFC/16-33-415

©
Mixed Sources
Product group from well-managed
forests, and other controlled sources
www.fsc.org Cert no. TT-COC-002641
© 1996 Forest Stewardship Council
FSC

This book is made entirely of chain-of-custody materials

This book is dedicated to and
inspired by my darling grandchildren,
Joseph and Emily
who I love beyond words.

Chapter One
Introducing the Doers

Mummy

Daddy

2

A long time ago when there wasn't any
televisions to watch, any computers to play with,
or central heating to warm your house, there
lived a very happy family called the Doers.

Joe

Emily

lucy

When it was winter and cold outside Mummy Doer would stoke the fire in the hearth (a sort of fireplace) and make sure that she would put some more coal on the fire to warm the kitchen.

PURR

The Doers were a lovely family; there was Mummy Doer, Daddy Doer, Joe and Emily Doer.

Once the kitchen was warm,
Mummy Doer would call the
children downstairs to come
and eat their breakfast.

They did not have a toaster, so
Mummy Doer would put great
thick chunks of home-made
bread on something called a
toasting fork and hold it over the low
flame until each side was golden brown.

She would spread butter and
homemade jam on the gorgeous
warm toast and smile as Joe
and Emily munched their
delicious breakfast.

Daddy Doer had milked the cow, and the warm milk was then poured into a yellow cup for Joe and a pink cup for Emily.

The milk was as fresh as you could imagine.

The two children drank every drop and looked as contented as pussy cats as the last drop disappeared.

The Doers did not have a lot of money to spend so they did most things themselves.

In the next chapters you will find out how many things they could do.

lap
lap

The Doers lived very simply.

They did not have a lot of things.

Daddy Doer would sell eggs, milk, vegetables and fruit to the neighbours.

They had chickens in the garden.

The chickens provided gorgeous large eggs.

Every day the eggs were gathered and taken into the house so that Mummy could add them to her cakes, make omelettes or simply boil them.

She cut bread into thin slices, so that Joe and Emily could dip the bread into the yolk and suck and chew the scrummy soft meal.

The back garden was very large, not all laid out, very functional which means a place where you could easily do whatever you needed to do.

They had one cow, three big trees – one apple, one pear and one plum – a big vegetable patch where they grew carrots, turnips, potatoes, onions, cabbage and all types of vegetables.

They grew herbs, to flavour the food. They had lavender bushes so they could pick and dry the lavender. Mummy would place the tiny mauve flowers in a bowl which would make the inside of the house smell wonderful.

There was another part of the garden where pretty flowers grew.
Mummy Doer would pick a bunch of flowers every week when they were in bloom.

She would get a vase, fill it with water, and carefully arrange roses, tulips or daffodils, depending on the season.
Of course, Emily would help.

That would brighten the hallway as you entered the Doers' happy, happy home.

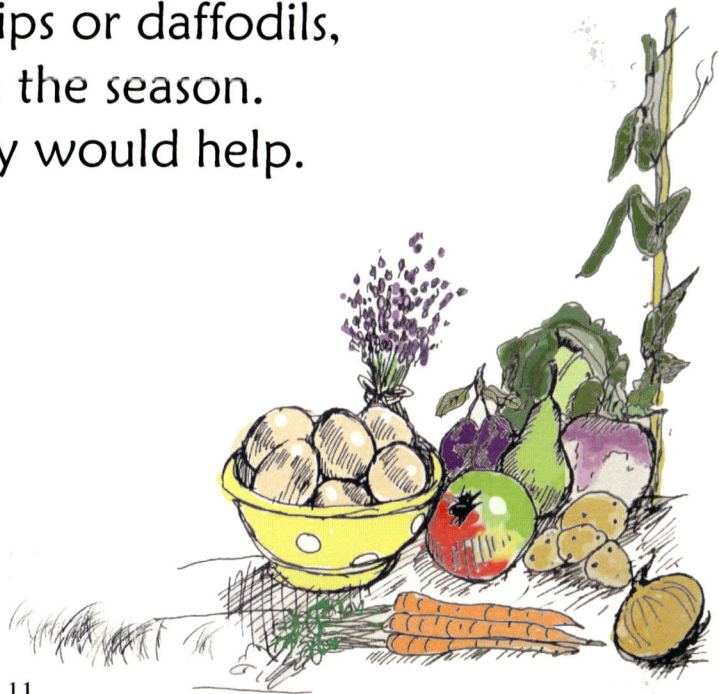

Daddy Doer spent lots of
time in the shed at the bottom of the
garden with Joe.

He would teach Joe how to make things
out of wood.

He would teach Joe how to use a saw, a
hammer and nails.

They had started to make a cupboard.

In the next chapter I will tell you if
the cupboard was actually made.

Chapter Two
Hammers and Nails

Joe and Daddy Doer were in the shed.

It was cold, so they were wrapped up nice and warm.

There was an oil heater in the corner,
but it only slightly took the chill off the shed.
Joe loved going to the shed with Daddy.

They always made things.

He was told to be very careful and shown
how to use tools without having any accidents.

Daddy had different pieces of wood
leaning up against the wall, the outside of
the cupboard, the doors and the shelves.

On the work bench there were screws, nails and
small tools, screwdrivers and a small hammer.

Daddy had these tools set out so that it was easier for Joe.

They spent many hours making the cupboard; Daddy did the hard bits and Joe helped with the smaller tasks.

Eventually the cupboard was finished.

It had taken a long time, but it had been such fun actually making something.

They had been very busy.

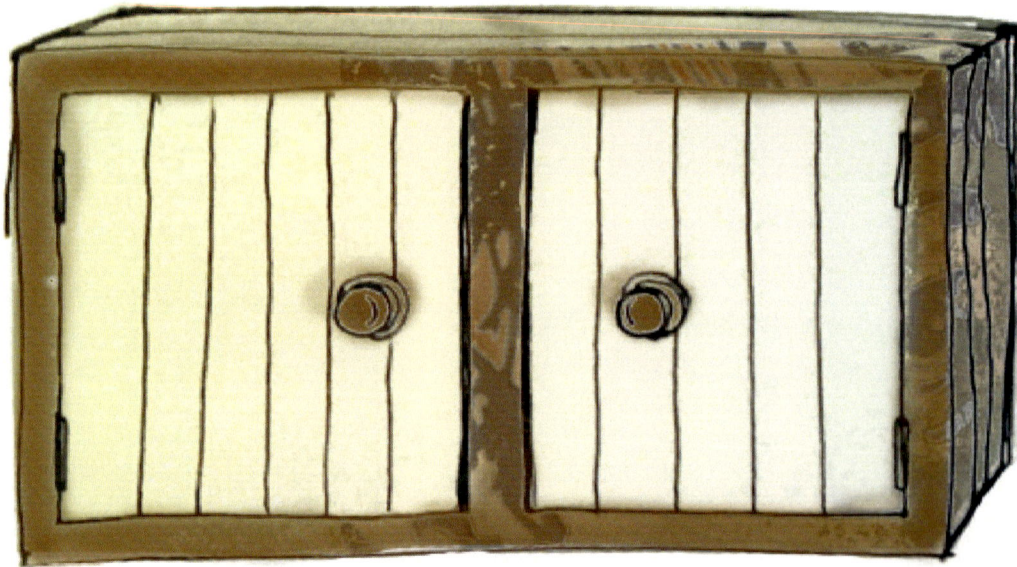

They both agreed it was time to go back into the house to see Mummy and Emily, have a lovely warm drink and some biscuits.

Daddy and Joe walked hand in hand down the path, their hot breath making little clouds of smoke as they walked in the cold winter air.

Joe's dad suggested that tomorrow he would paint the cupboard and asked Joe if he would like to help.

Joe smiled, and nodded yes. He was having a very happy day.

Mummy Doer was filling the tin
bath with hot water so that the
children could have a good
soak before bedtime.

They did not have a bath every day
but at least once or twice a week.

It was quite difficult for Mummy.

She had to keep boiling water and carrying
it across the kitchen to the fireside and then
she had to get cold water so that the
children would be able to soak in a comfortable
temperature – not too hot and not too cold.

Joe and Emily always had their bath together.

They couldn't splash too much,
but they did have a great time.

Mummy Doer used to sing funny little songs like

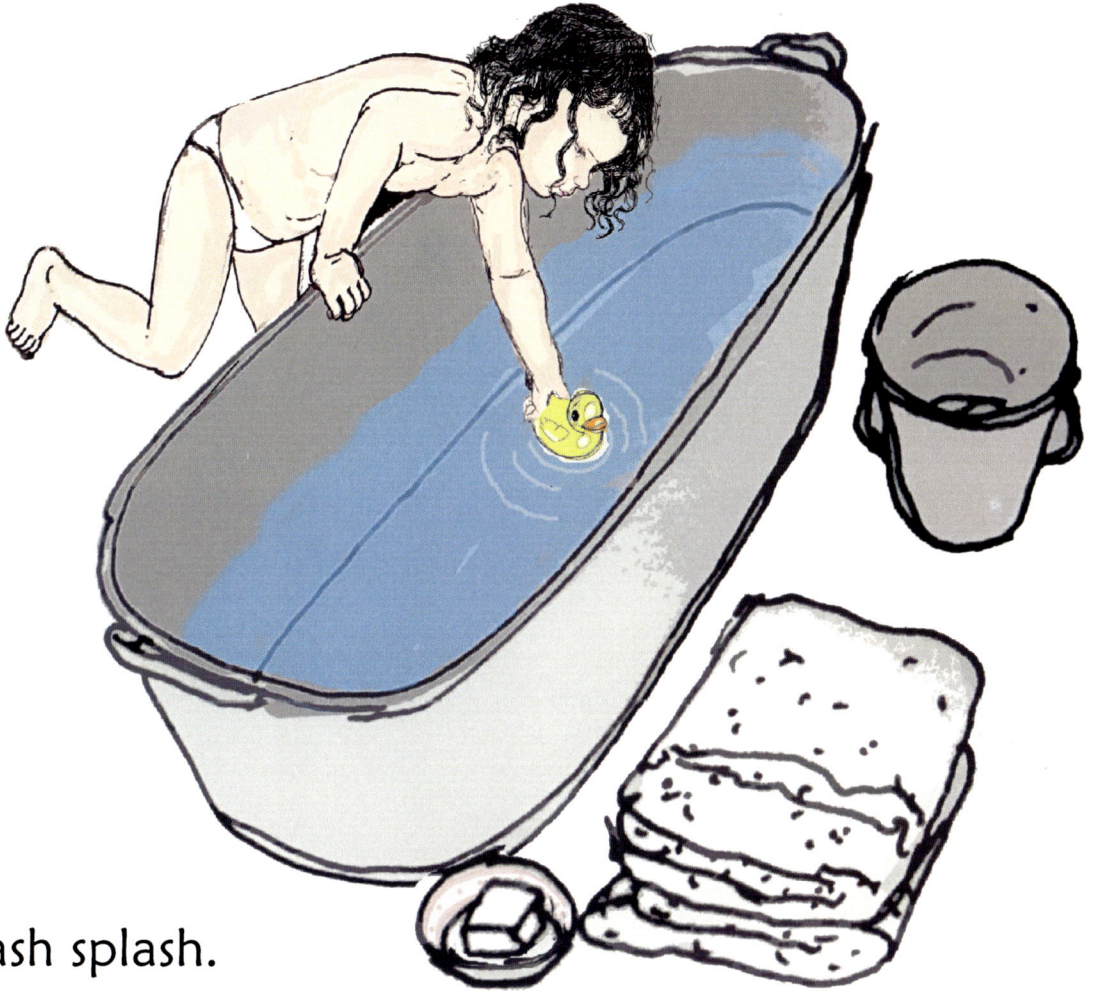

'Splash splash.
All of a dash.
Now you are all clean.
Once you have brushed your teeth from top to toe.
You'll surely gleam.'

Every night she would change the song slightly.
Mummy Doer loved to sing.

Mummy Doer had two great big towels
she would hold them in front of the fire so
that they would be all snuggly and warm as
Emily and Joe got out of the bath.

Emily and Joe would then have something
to eat, a hot drink and go to bed.

Joe was looking forward to painting
the cupboard with Daddy.

In the next chapter we will see if they do.

Chapter Three
A Rainbow

The Doers had all had a good night's sleep.

They had gone to bed when it got dark
and the moon and stars were shining and
got up as soon as they could see
daylight and hear the birds tweeting.

Today was the day that Daddy and Joe
Doer were going to paint the cupboard.

The cupboard was going to go in the kitchen so
that all the plates and cups and saucers could be
out of sight, neat and tidy. The question was which
colour they should paint the cupboard.

They had a cream-coloured paint, and a brown-coloured
paint. Daddy and Joe could not make up their minds.

'I know,' said Joe. 'Let's paint the top and
bottom of the cupboard brown,
the inside shelves cream, the front
cream and the sides brown.'

'That sounds a good idea, said Daddy.

It was all going very well until Daddy turned
round to get a clean paint brush and knocked
his pot of cream paint onto the floor.

Although it was not all that funny Joe giggled; it was the
look on Daddy Doer's face which made him laugh.

Daddy did not laugh at first, but looked rather cross.
Then, seeing and hearing Joe laughing so loudly,
he started to smile, then he grinned and then
he started to laugh out loud.

Then he laughed so much.
In fact, Joe and Daddy laughed until
they could laugh no more.

It was so funny.

I wonder what they are going to do next. Would they
clear the paint up, as best they can from the floor?
Would they let it all dry in a splodge?

After all, it was only the shed.
Or was there anything else they could do?

The paint had gone all over the stone
shed floor – a splish here, a splosh there.

Daddy Doer suggested that he get
some cleaning fluid to clean the
floor but Joe, who was very clever,
could see another hour or
so of enjoyment to be had.

Instead of having a dull grey stone floor
he thought it could be made into
something interesting to look at,
a sort of play area.

There was a shelf in the corner of the
shed and balanced upon the shelf were
empty plant pots – small ones,
big ones and middle-sized ones.

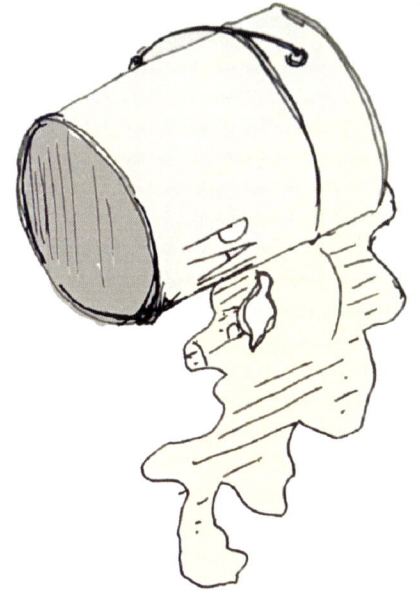

He thought if Daddy would reach up and get the plant pots, he could turn them over and press the rims into the wet paint to make all different size circles, and on days when there wasn't anything better to do, Emily and Joe could use colouring crayons or paint and turn the circles into faces, flowers, bumble bees or anything, a sun or a moon, so many different things.

Joe told Daddy his idea, and Daddy
Doer agreed that it was brilliant.
He smiled at Joe and ruffled his hair, telling
him he was such a clever little fellow.
Joe felt all warm and happy inside.
His Daddy was so kind; he was such a happy little boy.

As they made their way back to the
house it was just starting to rain
but the sun was shining.

Joe looked up to the sky and there,
high in the sky, was the most beautiful rainbow.

It seemed to curve over their house
like a great big bridge, a bridge of
wonderful colours, like a paint box in the sky.

They both stopped walking for a second
just to look at this amazing sight, then
went into the house to tell Mummy and Emily.

The four of them went into the garden
and just gazed up at the rainbow;
it was too beautiful for words.

For a whole minute they all stood silent and
then Mummy Doer said, 'All those
wonderful colours in the rainbow
have given me a good idea.

How about if tomorrow
we make a patch work quilt?'

Shall we see if they do?

lap
lap

Chapter Four
A Wonderful Present

Tomorrow came and
the sky was grey.
The wind was blowing;
rather a good day for
doing something inside.

Mummy Doer had a large box of all
sorts of coloured materials, left-overs
from skirts, shirts, curtains and cushion
covers that she had made previously.

The material had dots, stripes and floral patterns.

There were pieces of red, blue,
green – every colour you could think of.

Some of the materials were quite soft
and some were quite stiff.

Joe and Emily could not wait to
start making their patchwork quilt.

They had decided that they were going to
give it to Granny Doer for her birthday.

Granny Doer was a very old lady and would get very
excited even if you gave her a single flower, so probably
would jump with joy when she saw the wonderful quilt,
all finished and ready to keep her warm at night.

Mummy Doer showed Emily and Joe how to stitch the
material together; they did not have to match the colours
or the patterns. That was the way you
made this type of quilt.

They carefully cut the material and found all the cotton
that they needed to enable them to sew the pieces
together. It took ages to get the cotton through
the small eye of the needle.

Mummy showed them how.
They made the end of the cotton wet which made it easier
and after a couple of goes the cotton was threaded.
Mummy gave everybody a thimble to put on their fingers.

A thimble was like a tiny, little
silver-coloured metal hat which fitted
over the top of your nail,
shaped like a policeman's helmet.

It protected you from pricking yourself. It took ages to make the quilt but the time went
quickly, as whilst they were sewing they listened to something called a wireless, which we now call a radio.

The wireless had lovely children's programmes.
One was called Listen with Mother.
A lady would say, 'Are you sitting comfortably?

Then we will begin.' She would then tell a story.
Sometimes they would hear something called Sparky's Magic Piano. It was all about a piano which did not only play music, but could also talk.
Imagine a talking piano!

The quilt took many weeks to finish. Every grey day they would do a little bit more and a little bit more until one day it was ready.

Joe, Emily, Mummy and Daddy each took a corner and placed it carefully on the floor.

It was so colourful, so interesting to look at. They all agreed that Granny would think it was the best present she had ever had. Money could not buy all the time and love that had been spent sewing the quilt.

They folded the quilt and wrapped it in brown paper, tying it with a thick satin red bow.

They placed it in the corner of the kitchen where it would stay until Granny Doer's birthday.

We will wait with excitement; it will be very funny to see Granny jumping for joy. Let's see if she does.

Chapter Five

The Birthday Party

The day of Granny Doer's birthday
was here, although Granny had not yet arrived.

The party that the Doers were
making for her was a surprise.

Daddy Doer was busy blowing up balloons.
Joe and Emily were laughing because his face
was getting so red, almost as red as the balloon.

His cheeks were puffed out and he
had so many to blow up they
were hoping that he wouldn't run out of puff.

Joe and Emily were helping Mummy put the
finishing touches to the birthday cake.

They had made marzipan flowers and were placing them
on the top of the delicious sponge cake.

They then helped to make sandwiches and
when Mummy wasn't looking at them, had
a nibble of cucumber or
any other filling that was near.

Then Mummy got out her special
tablecloth, which she only used
for very special days and placed it on the kitchen table.

All the food was then arranged on
the best china, which was also only
used on very special days.
Everything was fine.

All they then had to do was to get
out their best party clothes.
Joe wore a sailor suit; which made
him look so grown up.
Emily had a lovely party dress, all
pink and frilly, with a big pink bow in her hair.
Daddy wore his new grey jumper
with matching trousers, and Mummy Doer
took her pinafore off, which was
very unusual.
She wore a nice green
dress with white dots on it.
She looked very pretty.

They were all ready to greet Granny Doer,
but where was she?

The clock on the wall was ticking.

Granny Doer was nowhere to be seen, had she got lost?

Had she missed her bus?

We will find out very soon.

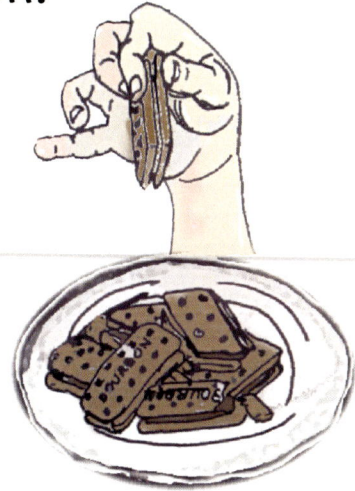

Thank goodness!

After only a short while there was a knock at the door.

It was Granny Doer, her grey hair tied back in a bun. She was wearing all her best visiting clothes.

Her face was old but so smiley, she was the kindest Granny and everybody was so pleased to see her.

She lived quite a way away.
They had to get on two buses to visit her.

As usual, Granny had come with gifts, home-made cakes that were simply delicious; nobody could make cakes like Granny. She had knitted scarves and hats for Emily and Joe, Mummy and Daddy, all matching.

They hugged and kissed and Granny was so happy to see all the balloons and the lovely table full of food.

She said they shouldn't have gone to all that trouble, but everybody secretly knew she was very pleased. The two children gave her the present they had taken so long to make.

Granny pulled at the ribbon and opened the paper, when she saw the quilt she had the biggest smile on her face.

She was really surprised and delighted.

She said that this was the most thoughtful, best
and most wonderful birthday present she
had ever had and she would keep it forever.

And, with that, she gave a little jump for joy, clapping her
hands. She did look funny; everybody laughed.

The food was eaten, the candles that
had been placed on the cake were lit and
Granny blew them out after making a wish.

Everybody sang 'Happy Birthday'; they were
all having such a great time.
Joe and Emily were getting very tired;
it had been a wonderful day.

Granny had to leave, in time to catch the last bus.
Mummy had put her present in a bag and Daddy
was going to help Granny carry it to the bus stop.

As they kissed and waved Granny goodbye, they
promised her that they would visit her soon.

In the next book we will see if they do.